Success Cloning

*The Ultimate Guide To Copy The
Success Secrets Of The Top 1%*

Deanna Cosso

Romuald Andrade

Publishing Services Provided by

 Archangel Ink

ISBN: 1532792549
ISBN-13: 978-1532792540

YOUR FREE GIFT

As a way of saying, "Thanks for your purchase," We are offering a free download of the ebook "Wake Up Successful - How to Increase Your Energy & Achieve Any Goal with a Morning Routine."

Getting unstuck is a real problem for a lot of people. The trick is to identify what you need to get done, and create a step-by-step strategy to launch your day so you execute your tasks in the most efficient way possible.

In "Wake Up Successful," you'll discover several ways to launch your day with a tried and tested morning routine. This will enable you to make lasting changes to your work, success, health, and sleep habits.

You can download this free ebook by going here:
http://7bigrocks.com/mr

Table of Contents

Chapter 1

Stunned, Sue sat frozen and speechless in front of Paul. She tried to take in what he was saying, but was barely able to focus as her mind struggled to comprehend what was happening.

"So you see," her boss continued, hands spread across his desk in a gesture of helplessness, "if this behavior persists, I won't be able to keep you on board. It isn't fair to the other realtors, and it certainly isn't fair of you to put me in this situation."

Paul sat back in his chair, crossed one leg over the other, and linked his fingers together in his lap as he waited for Sue's response.

Sue blinked, but didn't immediately respond. How could Paul possibly think she was capable of doing something so unprofessional? Actually, "unprofessional" was too kind. What Paul was accusing her of was downright shady!

"Sue?" His facial expression suddenly transformed from irritated to concerned, Paul uncrossed his legs and leaned forward. "Are you alright?"

Realizing she still hadn't spoken, Sue shook herself out of her state of shock. "Paul," she hesitated, still not believing what he had just said to her, "I just.." Taking a deep breath, Sue again shook her head, sat back in her chair, and tried to calm herself down as her mind became a dark, swirling void of unanswered questions.

Gripping the arms of the chair in an attempt to retain some grasp on reality during this most surreal moment, Sue exhaled. "Explain it to me again, Paul. I'm having trouble comprehending this. Tell me exactly what it is you think I did."

Sitting up a bit straighter, Paul cleared his throat. "Basically, the accountant wasn't able to accurately tally the sales for last month. As you know, when realtors sell a property, the paperwork they are required to complete for the sale is found and keyed in the computer database. At that time, the computer automatically enters the sale into the system. Once the sale has been completed in its entirety and the realtor submits it, the program automatically divides the realtor's commission between the realtor who sold the property, the broker, the listing agent, and the listing agent's broker."

"Right," Sue nodded. Obviously, she knew how commissions were split, and she had been working with this particular company long enough to understand how their software worked. What she didn't understand was what Paul thought she was guilty of doing.

"Ok," Paul nodded. "In addition to the mainframe, we have two backup systems," he explained, holding up two fingers on his right hand. "They're mostly just security in case the mainframe goes down, so we don't lose everything if the system crashes."

Sue again nodded, unclear as to where Paul was going with this.

"When Gary was trying to tally sales and commissions for last month," Paul continued, "the numbers didn't crunch. For some reason, the system shows our inventory as down by nine properties, but only eight appeared as having been sold. Also, the computer estimates the commissions we should be looking at each month, based not only on sales, but paperwork that's been completed. Unless a realtor cancels out all of the paperwork, essentially making it impossible to sell the property, the program recognizes it as a sale, even if the realtor doesn't submit it. The system was showing a much higher amount made in commissions, but the funds weren't there."

Trying to absorb this information, Sue knit her brow and tilted her head. "So there was a glitch with the system?"

"That's what we thought at first," Paul shook his head. "Then someone suggested we check the backup system to see if we could find any additional information." Looking down, her boss seemed embarrassed to go on. "Sue," he raised his eyes to hers, "the backup showed the missing property. It was yours. "

"I don't understand," Sue shook her head.

Looking at her sadly, Paul explained, "Another employee informed us that after you sold the property, you didn't submit the paperwork; rather, you deleted it once all was said and done on your part. The only reason for someone to do that would be to avoid splitting the commission."

By now, Sue's mouth was all but hanging open. Her eyes huge in disbelief, she felt her fingernails dig into the arms of the chair. Not trusting her voice at that moment, Sue closed her eyes tightly, and took a moment to compose herself. She could feel the tears creeping in behind her closed lids, and the last thing she was going to do was cry at work. Not after all the years of working so hard to be taken as seriously as her male counterparts. Not after having to work three times harder than the men in the office, just to be seen. While they all sat around drinking coffee and talking sports with the boss, she was busy finding leads and upping her game, just to try to get Paul to take notice of her work.

Taking a deep breath in an attempt to steady her racing heart, Sue opened her eyes. Her strained voice whispered, "I don't understand how you think I could do such a thing."

"Well," Paul sighed, "I have a very dependable source who keeps me apprised of the goings on in this office. I was disappointed and more than a little shocked to hear this about you. I was hoping you might have a good explanation, but then I realized there really is no acceptable explanation for your behavior."

"Excuse me?" Sue gasped. Forget being astounded and hurt by Paul's accusations. Now she was downright angry. "How long have I worked for you, Paul?" she demanded as leaned forward, fire in her dark eyes. "Have you *ever* known me to be anything less than the consummate professional?"

"No," Paul agreed, "You've been an outstanding worker up to this point. That's why I'm so dismayed by what I'm hearing." Paul looked down and adjusted his tie nervously. "Sue," he continued, returning his gaze to hers, "I understand we all make mistakes. This is a tough business. Sometimes we lose sight of the big picture, and do whatever it takes to succeed without taking into consideration the consequences. But we can't have that behavior in this office. We're better than that. *You're* better than that. Our reputation as a top real estate agency depends on the integrity and ethics of our employees. Once we lose that, we lose everything."

With an elbow on the arm of her chair, Sue lowered her head to her hand and applied pressure to her left temple, hoping to relieve the pressure of the headache she had developed in the past five minutes.

"Alright," Sue sighed, lowering her hand and raising her head to again confront Paul and his ghastly accusations. "These are some pretty serious charges. If you're going to believe them, you at least owe me an explanation as to why. I want to know where they came from. Who is this so-called 'very dependable' source whose word you believe over mine?"

"Oh no," Paul shook his head and fidgeted nervously, picking up the pen on his desk and rolling it between his fingers. "I can't break that person's confidence."

"Paul," Sue admonished, waiting for him to look her in the eye. "You *cannot* accuse me of something like this and refuse to tell me where it's coming from. If nothing else, out of respect for the years of work I've given you. Out of respect for *me* as a person, for God's sake, Paul. You owe me at least that."

Again, Paul broke eye contact and focused on the calendar on his desk, playing with the frayed edge as he chewed the inside of his cheek.

After what seemed like an eternity, Paul finally looked up at Sue. "Alright," he whispered, unsure of his position, but seeming to understand Sue's need to know. "Jim told me."

There it was. The black swirls in the dark void of her mind had returned as she attempted to process this information. Sue could feel her mouth open at Paul's admission, but no sound came forth. "Jim," she thought to herself as the pounding in her head amplified. "Jim."

Chapter 2

Even though it was six months ago, Sue remembered Jim's first day with the company like it was yesterday. He had blown into the office like a cool autumn breeze, with his fresh faced looks and sunny disposition. He'd worn a dark blue suit, which had brought out his eyes, and his sandy hair had been slightly tousled, as if he'd driven with the windows down. Sue had liked him immediately.

Knowing Paul was coming in a bit late that morning, Sue had taken it upon herself to welcome Jim to the office. She had introduced herself, and shown him to his workstation. Once he had put down his things, Sue had given him a quick tour of the office, showing him first to the copy room at the back of the office, and then to the break room, offering him a cup of coffee which he had gratefully accepted. As they had continued their rounds, Sue had introduced Jim to each realtor in the office, the accountant, and finally to Kim, the company secretary.

"Make sure you stay on Kim's good side," Sue had joked. "She's the one who orders all of our supplies, so if you want to stay stocked in printer cartridges and highlighters, you'll bring her a cup of coffee now and then."

"I think I can manage that," Jim had smiled.

Kim had shaken her blonde curls and laughed. "I'm not that bad!"

Smiling, Jim had raised his cup of coffee as if in a toast. "I'll be back later with the goods."

Laughing, Sue and Jim had made their way back to his work area. On the way, Sue had asked what had caused Jim to leave his previous job. He'd explained it was a very large firm, and commissions were split among all realtors, leaving the best sellers with little money left when all was said and done. Even though he was new to the real estate game, Jim had quickly become one of the top realtors in the office. After two years, Jim had decided he could do better in a smaller office.

"Thanks for the tour, Sue. Seems like a nice bunch of people."

"They are," Sue had agreed. "I'll think you'll fit in well."

Sue had been right on the money. Jim had become an absolute superstar in the office. Not only was he charismatic with his easy personality and quick smile, but he was knocking it out of the park workwise as well. Having brought a number of loyal clients with him from his previous office, he seemed never to be short of customers. Not to mention, in just a matter of weeks, he had already developed a supply of new contacts, most of which seemed to be panning out.

Ordinarily, a new realtor coming into the office and experiencing such success right off the bat might rub some of the old timers the wrong way, but Jim's lighthearted nature seemed to counteract any jealousy or ill will that might have been directed toward him. He had become an asset to the office in many ways, and was truly a breath of fresh air.

About the same time Jim was getting settled into the office, Sue had received a call from her younger cousin Joey who was once again in need of a job. It wasn't that Joey was a bad kid; quite the contrary. He was a hard worker, and always appreciative of any work he was given. Sue couldn't quite pinpoint what the issue was, but for some reason, he was never able to hold down a job.

On this particular occasion, Joey had been on his way to work when his car had broken down, as it so often had in the past. Unable to afford a rental, Joey had missed work for a few days while the car was being fixed. Upon his return to work, his boss had sat him down for a one on one. He had told Joey that while he was a good worker, he needed someone more reliable, and had let him go.

"I'm sorry Joey," Sue had comforted him, "I know you liked that job. Wasn't there a way for you to hitch a ride with someone else for a few days?"

"I know," Joey had replied. "I tried, but I couldn't find anyone going that direction. None of my coworkers lived anywhere near me, and I didn't want to put anyone out. I thought about taking a cab, but man.. I don't have that kind of money."

Sue had understood. Even if he'd called her for a ride, she likely wouldn't have been able to help him out. She'd either been needed at the office every morning, or had agreed to meet with clients first thing. "Funny," Sue had thought to herself, "how something as simple as transportation, something most people take for granted, can make the difference between keeping and losing a job."

Joey had been so hopeful, asking if Sue could possibly help him get into the real estate business. He'd figured because he had a degree in sales, he could transfer his skills into selling property. Sue had felt awful bursting his bubble, but she'd explained that a reliable vehicle is an integral part of succeeding in real estate. Disappointed, Joey had understood and acknowledged he wouldn't be able to invest in dependable transportation until he got a job making more money. Sue had told him she would think about some options for him, and touch base with him again soon.

The day after talking to Joey, Sue had met her two best friends, Jenna and Liz, for their usual Friday evening margaritas. For years, Sue and the girls had been making a point of getting together at least once a week to keep up with each other's busy lives. Liz worked some crazy hours managing a large department store, but always seemed to make time to meet up with her friends. Jenna, slightly older than Sue and Liz, was also in the realty business. In fact, Jenna was the reason Sue had initially become interested in the profession. Jenna was a wealth of knowledge and throughout the years had proven to be more than a good friend to Sue; she had become somewhat of a mentor.

A few years ago, Jenna had taken the leap and opened her own realty company. Jenna was the only realtor in the office, and she loved working for herself. She had told Sue she was welcome to come aboard and work with her at any time, and Sue had appreciated Jenna's faith in her immensely. Of course, Sue had always worried about mixing work and friendship. At the time, Sue had barely had a fraction of Jenna's experience, and wanted to be sure she could pull her own weight if she were ever to join her friend in her endeavors. Regardless, Jenna continued to be an invaluable mentor to Sue, and a cherished friend. She didn't know what she would do without her close female relationships.

Another important relationship in Sue's life was the one she had with her grandfather, Vito. As a child, Sue had always been close with her family, but she had formed a particularly special bond with her grandfather. Throughout her adult years, he had become her confidante, and when she found herself struggling, he offered her better advice than anyone else ever could.

Sue made it a point to visit her grandfather at least once a week, and the week Joey had called, she had confided in Vito during her visit. Vito had been long aware of Joey's difficulties in keeping a job, and wasn't surprised to hear the latest news. Vito's advice to Sue was to talk to Steve, her fiancé, and see if he could offer any help.

Sue had considered discussing Joey's predicament with Steve, but wasn't sure it was a good idea, only because Steve at times seemed annoyed by Joey's work history. Sue had tried to explain that the frequent job changes weren't really his fault, but Steve seemed to believe otherwise. Anyway, hearing Vito's suggestion had convinced Sue that discussing it with Steve was a good idea, no matter how he responded. At least she would be able to tell herself she had done all she could for Joey, even if it didn't lead to anything promising.

Being a manager at Mobile Tech, Steve supervised a group of engineers who created and tested new phone apps. Sue wasn't quite sure what type of work Joey could do at his company, but she had run it by him anyway. Surprisingly, Steve hadn't been judgmental of Joey when she'd filled him in on the situation. He'd actually seemed understanding, but made it clear that Joey would have no place in his company as his degree wasn't in engineering. However, Steve had immediately thought of his friend Sean.

Sean had been Steve's friend, and also his mentor. In fact, Sue thought to herself, they had a very similar relationship as she and Jenna. The difference was that Sean and Steve had actually worked together, and Sean had made an enormous impact in Steve's life. Sean had taught Steve organizational skills, and had thereby completely overhauled Steve's work practices. More importantly in Sue's eyes, Sean had taught Steve to carry those practices over to his personal life, and their relationship had never been better.

Steve had explained to Sue that Sean had started a successful new business on the east coast, and was in the process of expanding to the Los Angeles area. He thought perhaps Sean might be able to find a place for Joey, since he hadn't yet started hiring sales people. Steve had further suggested it would be helpful for Joey to have Sean as a mentor.

"Yes," Sue had agreed with Steve. "It would do Joey a world of good to learn from Sean."

Almost immediately, Steve had placed a call to Sean.

Thrilled with the opportunity to help his old friend, Sean had offered Joey a job, and Joey had soon been on his way to the east coast to train with him.

While feeling good about helping Joey, Sue had noticed her own work life was in a rapid decline. As the housing market had hit a bit of a rough spot, leads were fewer and further between.

The few leads Sue was getting seemed to be weaker, and they seldom converted to sales. Sue also noticed her coworkers snapping at each more, usually accusing one another of stealing clients and other unethical behavior.

Through all of the office politics, Sue had remained grateful for Jim's happy go lucky nature. Unlike others in the office, he never seemed to entertain the negativity, and was often able to break up office tension through his good humor. Sue wished she could be more like Jim and let things roll off of her as easily as he did.

Of course, Sue had noticed that Jim also didn't seem to be experiencing the backlash of a tough economy the same way the others were. He'd continued to have leads through it all, and didn't seem to be concerned about the declining market. Sue had assumed he was still cruising along on the leads he'd brought with him from his last job. Besides, with his personality, Sue knew people were attracted to him. Sue figured for every lead he had, they referred him to 10 others. He was just that sort of a person.

One evening, Sue had stayed late at the office to create some flyers, advertising her services. By around 7:15 pm she had finished them, and was walking to the back of the office to use the copy machine. As she walked past the break room, Sue had thought she'd heard someone in there; movement of some kind.

Surprised anyone else was still in the office at that hour, Sue had made a detour, and decided to poke her head into the break room to see who else was around. Upon opening the door, Sue almost jumped. She had caught a very surprised Kim and Jim in a compromising position. As they turned toward Sue and tried to compose themselves, the wheels in Sue's head had started spinning. Suddenly, it had occurred to her why Jim hadn't had any trouble finding clients. Kim, being in charge of dispersing the leads among the realtors, was clearly giving Jim the good contacts!

Although Sue had quickly exited the break room and the incident had never been addressed, Sue had decided to keep the secret to herself. While she fully understood what Jim and Kim were doing was unethical, and certainly harmful to the others in the office, her non-confrontational personality won out, and she simply wasn't comfortable discussing the situation with them, or even taking it to Paul to handle. No, Sue had kept their little secret all to herself, hoping the problem would eventually go away. After all, since they had been caught, certainly they would feel the need to be more cautious and begin to do the right thing, wouldn't they? At least, that's what Sue had hoped would happen. Obviously, she had been wrong. So very wrong.

Chapter 3

Sue sat in stunned silence, her eyes barely focused, as she processed what Paul had just told her. "Jim," she thought to herself. After all she had done for him, starting with welcoming him to the office, and ending with keeping his and Kim's secret to herself.

"I must be an idiot," she whispered, finally shaking her head and coming back to the present day.

"I'm sorry?" Paul asked, head tilted and eyes filled with confusion.

Sue straightened up in her chair, readying herself for the conversation she knew they had to have.

"Paul," Sue began, "Do you honestly believe that after almost five years of working for you, I would one day wake up and decide it was time to try to cheat the system? Obviously I haven't been paid the commission from my last sale yet. If I had, I would have noticed the commission hadn't been divvied up, and I would have reported it to accounting."

Paul shook his head. "Jim showed me what you did, Sue. Computers don't lie, and.."

'Paul," she interrupted, holding up a hand and taking a deep breath. "I'm going to tell you something I should have told you a long time ago."

As Paul sat back in his chair, crossed one leg over the other and waited, Sue gathered her nerve.

"A few months ago, while working late, I stumbled upon Jim and Kim in the break room. I caught them in sort of a.. well, kind of an awkward position." Sue felt her face flushing as she tried to make her point without sounding crass.

Paul knit his brow, as if trying to absorb what Sue was saying.

"I think they've been seeing each other for a while," Sue continued. "At least, that's how it looked."

Paul began to fiddle with his tie, clearly uncomfortable with the conversation. "Kim is married, Sue," he said, still looking down at his tie. "I've met her husband. They seem happy. I find it hard to believe she would do something like that."

"Well, believe it," Sue responded. "I saw it with my own two eyes."

"Alright," Paul nodded, finally returning her gaze. "For the sake of argument, let's say it's true. What does that have to do with you?"

Raising her eyebrows, surprised that Paul wasn't putting it together, Sue realized she'd have to spell it out for him. "First of all, if you were having an affair and got caught by someone in the office, wouldn't you want them gone?"

Paul shook his head, as if about to argue, but Sue cut him off. "And as if being caught with your hand in the cookie jar weren't enough, there's more. Haven't you noticed almost every realtor in this office is having a tough time getting leads, lately?"

"Sure," Paul shrugged. "The housing market took a nosedive. It happens."

"Right. But haven't you also noticed that Jim seems to be doing just fine, through it all?"

"He's a hell of a realtor, Sue," Paul countered. "His people skills are unsurpassed. That always makes for excellent sales."

"I get that," Sue nodded. "But even with his skills and the contacts he brought with him from his last place, he's doing unusually well compared to everyone else. Think about it. Your top agents aren't holding a candle to him right now."

Paul uncrossed his legs, rolled his chair forward, and crossed both arms on the desk. "What exactly are you getting at?"

"Kim is the secretary. She answers the phone. When new clients call, Kim is the one who distributes them among the realtors. Until now, she's always done it on a rotation. We've always gotten at least a couple of new leads every week, even when the market has been slow. Suddenly, we're lucky to get a couple of new leads a month. Except for Jim. Somehow, new clients seem to keep rolling in for him."

"So what you're telling me is that because Kim is having an affair with him, you think she's giving all the new leads to Jim?"

"That's exactly what I'm telling you," Sue nodded. "She's giving him the strong leads, while the rest of us are getting the leftovers. Jim's leads seem to pan out more often than not, while ours tend to be more the 'looky loos'; people who want to see what's available in this market, but aren't planning to buy any time soon."

Paul sat back in his chair, closed his eyes, and wiped a hand down his face. Opening his eyes, he shook his head. "I don't know what's going on with you Sue, but to make an accusation like that.."

"Paul!" Sue gasped. "I'm telling you the truth! You must have noticed how successful he's been while the rest of us are struggling.."

Paul raised a hand and cut her off. "Look," he raised his voice. "I haven't heard complaints from anyone else. Apparently you're the only one who has a problem with him. He came in here, fit in well with everyone, and frankly, has done nothing but a great job since day one."

Sue's mouth opened slightly, but no sound escaped.

"I also find it odd that until now, you've made no mention of this so-called affair between Jim and Kim. Now that you're being called on the carpet, suddenly everyone is at fault but you, right?"

"Are you kidding me?" Sue exclaimed, hands open wide in front of her. "I've worked for you for years, and you believe this guy over me? A guy who's been here less than a year? I have never given you a single reason to doubt my integrity!"

"No, you haven't," Paul agreed. "Not until now. Sue, I'm so disappointed. Clearly you're threatened by the level of success Jim has experienced in the short time he's been here, and you're doing everything you can to taint my image of him. This isn't like you, and it's unacceptable behavior from someone who is supposed to be a professional."

Clearly irritated, Paul continued. "I've seen this before. A new realtor comes in, and in a short time, surpasses all of the agents who have been at the job for years. It makes for an uncomfortable situation, I get that. But you can't go around making up lies and setting people up for failure just because you're threatened."

"Look, Sue," Paul lowered his voice and put on his "mentor" hat. "The best way to deal with this is to give 110%. Try to learn from Jim and model his behavior. Hell, ask him to show you what he's doing to be so successful in this market. He's a good guy. I have no doubt he'll take some time with you and show you the ropes. Use him as a resource, Sue. Instead of trying to sink him, get on his side and soak up all you can from him."

By now, Sue was shaking with anger. Trying to keep herself in check, she stood up, her face red with fury. In an attempt to control herself, Sue spoke deliberately, but passionately. "If this is how you see me, then clearly there is nothing left to say." Sue spun on her heel and began to walk out of Paul's office.

As she put her hand on the doorknob, she turned toward Paul one last time. "No, there is something else. As far as being disappointed, I never thought you could disappoint me the way you have just now. I'd have thought the past five years would have meant something to you, the way they have to me. Now I realize, you never took the time to get to know me at all. Some new Joe comes in and charms the office, rubs up to you with all of his sports talk and does what he can to become one of the guys, and all of my hard work and loyalty to you is forgotten."

Sue took a breather and looked at Paul with his elbows on his desk, mouth resting against his joined hands, and his eyes looking at something unseen.

"Maybe someday you'll realize the mistake you've made," Sue whispered. "Then again, maybe you won't. Either way, I won't be around to find out."

At that, Sue flung open the office door and stormed out. The last thing she saw as she hurried toward the front door was a very nervous looking Kim talking on her cell phone, glancing at her through the corner of her eye.

"To hell with all of them," Sue breathed as she reached her car. "I'm done with this crap. From now on, I work for myself."

Sue felt a sense of relief as she drove out of the parking lot. Yes, she realized. That was the answer. It was time to be her own boss.

Chapter 4

As soon as Sue walked through the door of the cozy, two bedroom home she shared with Steve, she threw her satchel on the coffee table and poured herself a glass of red wine. Kicking off her shoes, she flopped down on the sofa and took a long sip of her drink, savoring the fruity aroma and flavor as much as the mild numbing effect it had on her racing mind.

Since storming out of the office, all Sue had been able to think about was working for herself. She never again wanted to be in a position where so many years of hard work could go unrecognized, and a superior could so unfairly belittle her personal character. Of course, now that she was home and starting to calm down, she had to face the fact that she wasn't ready to open her own real estate company. Her five years of experience would serve her well no matter where she went, but to open a company of her own was to place herself in a different league entirely.

Jenna had opened her own real estate company a little over two years ago. Sue remembered watching the struggles Jenna had faced, and the seemingly never-ending stress that went with the territory. At the time, Jenna had at least ten years of experience as a realtor, and had a number of loyal clients who followed her to the new location. Even so, she had struggled with the day to day challenges that went along with learning how to run a business. Sue remembered Jenna's anxiety in deciding how to most wisely invest her money. Certainly, she had needed to position her company in an upscale area to attract a certain clientele, but doing so had meant committing to a much higher overhead than she had originally anticipated. In order to balance herself financially, this meant cutting back on office furnishings, accessories, and other little luxuries she would have liked. The end result was not the office of her dreams; rather, a functional, comfortable workspace. Jenna had even learned to do her own books to save on accounting fees, but did splurge on a part-time receptionist to lend an air of professionalism to the business.

No, Sue had neither the experience nor the finances to open an office of her own. Facing that reality, Sue again began to think about how when Jenna had finally gotten her company up and running, she had extended an invitation to Sue to come work with her anytime she'd like. Sue had never taken her up on her offer, only because she had been hesitant to become a business partner with one of her best friends. If business went sour, would the friendship go with it? Sue liked to think their friendship was strong enough to withstand any difficulties working together could bring, but knew she'd have to run it by Jenna and see if she felt the same way.

"Hey!" Sue's thoughts were interrupted by Steve bursting through the door. "I wasn't expecting you to be here."

"Hey," Sue smiled as Steve walked to the sofa to give her a kiss. "You're home early."

"Yeah. I had a lunch meeting with a client, and since it was on this side of town, I decided to finish out the day here. What about you? Anything good on the horizon?"

"Actually," Sue hesitated, watching as Steve poured himself a glass of wine and settled in next to her. "I quit my job today."

Steve froze, wine glass halfway to his lips. Blinking, he placed his glass on the coffee table, and then turned to face Sue, waiting for her to continue.

Sue stared into her wine glass, running a finger around the rim. "It's a long story, but I've been doing a lot of thinking. I think I'm ready to start working for myself. Well, not exactly by myself, though. I'm considering asking Jenna if I can start working with her."

"Wow," Steve nodded. "That's a big move."

"It is," she agreed. "But I need a change."

Again, Steve nodded. "Have you talked to Jenna about it?"

"Not yet. I'm pretty sure she'll agree to it. When she first opened her company, she had asked me if I wanted to come work with her."

"I remember."

"Well, I have the same concerns now that I had back then. I mean, it's hard to mix business with friendship. I don't want to disappoint her."

Steve brushed a strand of hair out of Sue's eyes. "You won't disappoint her. It'll be great to work so closely with her. Look at what working with Sean did for me. And on top of being an incredible mentor, he became one of my best friends."

"I guess. But this business is Jenna's baby. If I do something to bring her down.."

"You won't," Steve interrupted. "She'll be lucky to have you. When are you going to bring it up to her?"

"I haven't really gotten that far."

"I think you should call her now."

"Oh, I don't really know what I'm going to say yet.."

"Come on," Steve pressed. "You already said it. It's time for a change. Call her."

After another moment of hesitation, Sue nodded. Putting her glass on the coffee table next to Steve's, Sue reached for her bag and dug out her cell phone. She found the contact she was looking for, and sent a text:

Hi Jenna, do you have time to meet for dinner tomorrow? My treat.

The next evening, Sue and Jenna sat at one of their favorite meeting places, where the food was good and the margaritas were strong. After taking a sip of the frozen concoction in front of her, Jenna sat back, looked at Sue, and raised her drink in the air. "Alright, you lured me here with these luscious things in the middle of the week; there must be something on your mind."

"You got me," Sue laughed. "After yesterday, I really needed a drink.. and to vent to a good friend."

"That bad?" Jenna asked, eyebrows raised.

Focusing on the straw she was using to slowly draw circles in the icy slush, Sue nodded. "I quit my job yesterday."

Jenna's eyes grew large with surprise. "You're kidding! I thought you loved working there?"

"I thought so too," Sue said sadly. Looking up at her friend, she let out a sigh. "It's a long story, but I've decided I need to work for myself. I know my work ethic, and I believe I can do better on my own than working for another big company where they don't appreciate what I do."

"I hear that," Jenna nodded, taking another sip of her drink.

"Well, that's what I wanted to talk to you about," Sue began, taking a deep breath. "I remembered how when you started your company, you had asked if I would be interested in joining you."

"I remember," Jenna again nodded. "As I recall, you had some concerns about friends working together."

"Yes," Sue agreed, "And I still do, but I think I'd like to give it a try. That is, if the offer still stands."

"Of course it does," Jenna offered. "I think it's always scary for friends to go into business together, but as long as we keep communication open and let each other know if we have an issue with something the other is doing, I think we'll be alright."

"I think so too," Sue smiled; relieved her friend was still open to the idea. "I think my biggest concern is I don't have the amount of experience you do and because of that, I really don't have many clients that will follow me. It worries me that I may not be able to find enough leads right away to make ends meet."

"That will come with time," Jenna assured her friend. "Building a loyal client base is obviously one of the challenges of working for yourself, and one of the most important aspects of being successful. But the single most important thing is your work ethic, which includes your integrity, and I've seen you in action. Potential clients will pick up on that quickly, and know they're in good hands with you. There isn't a doubt in my mind you'll be an asset to the company."

"That means so much to me coming from you, Jenna," Sue said. "It's scary to think about branching out on my own. I'm so grateful for your faith in me. It makes it a little easier to know I'm not really on my own; that I have someone with so much experience as a mentor."

"Absolutely," Jenna agreed. "If you agree to it, I'd like to do the same thing we both did when we worked for larger agencies. We'll each work with our own clients, but we'll share commissions. I figure that'll help you with the transition. If it takes you a little longer to close some deals, at least you'll still have some money coming in."

"Thanks," Sue accepted, a bit hesitantly. "I just want to be sure I don't hold you back. It may take me some time to establish a network."

"Of course it will," Jenna nodded. "But I'll give you the names of some agencies realtors can pay to secure leads. It's a good way to get your feet off the ground when you're first starting out. But to give you a head start, I'm going to give you a few of the leads I've already bought. That way you can really hit the ground running."

"Wow, thanks!" Sue exclaimed. "I really appreciate that!"

"No problem," Jenna smiled. Then, raising her glass in the air, she toasted, "To our success!"

"To our success!" Sue returned, feeling more optimistic than she had in a long while.

Chapter 5

"No, I understand," Sue replied into the phone, blinking back the tears that were starting to fill her eyes. "Thanks anyway. If you know of anyone else interested in buying or selling, feel free to give them my card."

Sue hung up the phone and put her head in her hands. "What am I going to do?" she wondered. It had been over three months since she had begun working with Jenna, and she hadn't closed a single deal. As promised, Jenna had given her some of the leads she had purchased, but they hadn't panned out. Sue had gone on to buy her own leads, and none of those had worked out either.

Sue wiped the tears from her eyes, frustrated with herself for being so emotional, but also angry with the way things were turning out. Every lead had seemed so promising in the beginning. She had been sure she was going to have a long list of clients sooner than expected. But in time, each client had dropped out for different reasons. They either believed the asking price was too high for this slow economy, or they simply weren't finding what they were looking for.

"Damn," she whispered to herself, turning to her computer screen and pulling up her list of contacts. Each name, except for the very last, had "inactive" next to it, describing the current account status. Sue felt her stomach sink as she changed the status of the last name on the list from "active" to "inactive." She didn't have a single name on her list with the words "pending" or "sold" next to it.

Staring at the screen with unfocused eyes, the negative

thoughts that had been routinely invading Sue's mind over the past several weeks took over. "Face it," she thought to herself, "You're a colossal failure." As hard as Sue still tried to convince herself she had made the right move in leaving her job and coming to work with Jenna, she had her doubts.

On her better days, Sue tried to find reasons outside of herself for the struggle she was facing. For starters, the leads she was buying from other agencies were weak. Buying them was eating up her savings, and she hadn't been able to convert a single one into a sale. Obviously, agencies wouldn't sell their best leads; that wouldn't make any sense. They were only selling those that they knew wouldn't go anywhere; the leads nobody else wanted. What a game they were running! Even the leftover leads Sue had been getting at her old job were better than these!

As far as the contacts Jenna had given her, Sue didn't know what to think. None of them had led to a sale, but interestingly, Jenna didn't seem to have any problem converting her own leads into sales. Was it possible Jenna had deliberately given her weak leads? It made sense that Jenna would want to keep her best clients for herself, so maybe she had provided Sue with her less than desirable contacts, hoping she wouldn't know the difference.

Of course, when she sat down with her thoughts and examined her situation honestly, Sue knew there was more to it. Jenna was buying leads from the same agencies, and was as successful as ever. And obviously, Jenna would never set her up for failure. Sue knew the contacts Jenna had provided were as strong, if not stronger, than the ones she kept for herself. Such was Jenna's nature; she had always encouraged Sue, and wanted to see her succeed.

Clearly, Jenna's faith in her was a big part of Sue's disappointment in herself. Letting down Jenna, her mentor, was the last thing she had wanted to do. Jenna, being the true friend she was, remained gracious, encouraging Sue and telling her things would pick up. Sue didn't know how long Jenna would continue to be patient with her. After all, since Sue had started working with her, Jenna had made a few sales, and per their original agreement, had split her commissions with Sue. Sue felt she had contributed nothing in return, and knew that eventually this would strain their relationship.

Sue took a deep breath and ran her hands through her dark hair. Realizing she was sinking into depression, Sue made herself a promise. If she couldn't soon become an asset to Jenna's business, she would move on. Her financial struggles were becoming too much of a burden, but more importantly, she didn't want to become a burden to Jenna. Jenna's friendship was too important to lose. Sue had no idea what her next move would be, but she knew she would have to figure it out quickly. She shook her head and mumbled to herself, "This is it. You've got a few more weeks to show you can make it. If nothing changes, it's time to go."

With that, Sue grabbed her things and started the drive home. Frustrated after another long and unproductive day, she knew if she waited five more minutes, rush hour would be at its peak and her drive time would double. The last thing she needed right now was to get stuck in traffic. All she wanted was to get home and try to relax. Maybe once she was curled up on the sofa, glass of wine in hand, she would have a better perspective on things. She would take some time for herself tonight, and consider all of her options. Maybe she would make a list of pros and cons to help her decide whether working for herself was worth it, or if she should start looking to hire on with another big real estate firm. Maybe she would explore leaving real estate behind altogether. After all, she had plenty of sales experience by now; maybe she could turn her skills into a lucrative job with another corporation. "Alright girl," Sue tried to calm herself. "You need to remember you aren't boxed in. There are other things out there you can do. There's still time to start over."

Just as the gloom clouding Sue's mood was beginning to lift, she suddenly felt her car pull to the left. "What the heck," Sue gasped, trying to keep the vehicle straight on the road. Vibrating beneath her and becoming sluggish, she realized the car must have blown a tire. "Terrific," Sue grumbled as she pulled the car to the shoulder. "Just what I need today."

Coming to a stop, Sue killed the engine, turned on her hazards, and leaned back in the seat and closed her eyes. "Unbelievable," she whispered. "Just when you thought it couldn't get any worse."

After a moment, Sue took a deep breath, and stepped out of the car. Sure enough, the front driver's side tire had gone flat. Leaning against the car, Sue shook her head, her anxiety at a whole new level. "Now what," she mumbled. She had her cell phone, but Steve was at work on the other side of town. It would take him well over an hour to reach her. Jenna was out on calls all day, showing properties. No way was Sue going to interrupt her and possibly cost her a sale.

Just as she was regretting not having enrolled in Triple A, a car pulled to the side of the road next to her. As grateful as she was that someone had stopped to offer assistance, Sue's attention was more drawn to the car itself; a brand new, cherry red Porsche. "Wow," Sue exhaled.

She was still focused on the car, not noticing the driver had stepped out and was now calling to her. "Hey, Sue!" Joey yelled to her. "Talk about good timing!"

Sue stood blinking, momentarily dumbstruck. Joey? This was the same cousin who had come to her six months ago, asking for advice in keeping a job?

By now, Joey had come around the side of his car and was hugging her. "Good to see you," he said. "Sorry it isn't under better circumstances."

"Joey," Sue stammered. "I'm so glad to see you; you have no idea! Is this your car?"

"Yep," Joey smiled proudly. "Sorry I haven't had a chance to call you. I've been wanting to thank you and Steve for everything you've done for me."

"Sure looks like it worked out," Sue said, still in shock.

"Come on," Joey opened the passenger door to the Porsche. "I'll fill you in on the way home."

As Joey drove Sue home, he told her all about his new job. He raved about his time on the east coast, telling her how the training he had received from Sean during that time was the best learning experience he'd ever had.

"I'm telling you, Sue," Joey went on, "Nothing I learned in college even compares with the training Sean gave me. It was real life experience, you know? College is all theory. This was real, hands-on training. He taught me how to succeed at a job. Nobody had ever done that for me before."

"That's wonderful," Sue nodded. "And in six months you've already made enough to buy this car?"

Joey laughed. "No, not exactly." I was named the top salesperson in the region last quarter. The Porsche was the prize."

"Are you kidding me?" Sue gasped. "That's one hell of a prize!"

"I know!" Joey agreed. "I'm telling you Sue, Sean's business is legit! That dude is gonna be a millionaire by the time he retires, no doubt in my mind."

"Wow," Sue shook her head in awe. "Incredible. Well, I'm glad at least one of us is doing well."

Joey turned his head toward Sue. "What do you mean?"

Sue leaned her head against the headrest and again shook her head, staring at the ceiling of the car. "It's a long, awful story."

"Judging by traffic, we have plenty of time," Joey offered.

Joey's eyes grew large as Sue told him why she had quit her job at the real estate agency. As Sue went on to detail the issues she was having with her new business, Joey listened, carefully considering everything she said. Her financial troubles were reminiscent of the life he was living before his training with Sean. Sue was such a go-getter, it worried Joey that her self-esteem was taking such a beating; not to mention, her life savings. He began to ask why she hadn't asked Steve for help, but quickly bit his tongue. His cousin had always been fiercely independent, even as a kid, and instinctively he knew she wouldn't be comfortable asking anyone for help, not even her fiancé. No, Joey knew the only way to help Sue was the same way she had helped him.

"Sue," Joey began, "Why don't you ask Sean to teach you some of the same tactics he taught me? I mean, you're trying to make a go of your own business, right?"

"Right," Sue answered cautiously. "Well, it's my friend Jenna's business. She just invited me in. But yeah, we both work for ourselves; we just split commissions. Well, I mean, we will if I ever make any."

"Ok," he continued. "So you're pretty much in the same position Sean was in when he ventured out on his own."

"Not really," Sue snorted. "He was immediately successful."

"True," Joey nodded. "But that's only because he developed his skills before he went out on his own. Remember all the stuff he taught Steve about organization, and basically being more productive at work?"

"Yeah," she agreed. "And outside of work."

"Right." Joey pulled into Sue's driveway and stopped the car. "I think you should talk to Steve about having Sean help you. It worked for him, it worked for me.. I'm pretty sure it could help you, too."

Sue gathered her things and reached over to give her cousin a hug. "Thanks, Joey. I'll keep it in mind. Thanks for the ride. So glad to see you're doing well. I'll call you soon."

As Joey pulled away and Sue went into the house, her mind was spinning again. Between her and Steve, she had always been the organized one. She'd always had her stuff together, and been successful at her job. "No," she shook her head. "I can do this on my own. I don't need to get anyone else involved. I just need to buckle down and get serious."

Chapter 6

"Alright Ms. Martinez, thanks for the call. I have a pretty good idea of what you're looking for, so as soon as anything comes up in your price range, I'll let you know. Thanks again." Sue hung up the phone and let out a long sigh. "Yeah, right," she thought to herself. "I'm sure I'm going to find a four bedroom home in that price range. Good luck, Ms. Martinez."

Over a month had gone by since her car had broken down, and Joey had come to her rescue. Since their conversation, Sue had been determined to make a change in the progress of her career. She had begun purchasing leads from a new agency, where the leads were more expensive, but had an excellent rate of success. Although she'd had a few promising prospects, the trend continued, and so far nobody had committed to buying anything from her.

Unfortunately, the market wasn't helping. As the economy continued to decline, the competition for buyers was becoming fiercer. Even Jenna was having more trouble than usual closing deals, but at least she made a sale now and then.

Once again, Sue was becoming extremely discouraged. Worse than that, the guilt of not contributing to the agency was overwhelming. She knew it was only a matter of time before Jenna grew tired of being the only one selling property, and having to split her commissions with someone who was not holding up her end of the bargain.

Jenna was always kind, but Sue was sure she sensed a tinge of resentment in her. Well, why wouldn't she resent having to split her money with Sue. Until Sue came along, Jenna was doing just fine. True, Sue was doing her best to carry her half of the overhead they paid for the space, but that didn't make up for her lack of success. Jenna would have much more money in her pocket if she just paid for the space herself as she had been, and pocketed her full commissions. Sue had again started to worry about their friendship, knowing that eventually Jenna's patience would wear thin.

As Sue shut down her computer and prepared for the drive home, the same, familiar thought intruded her mind as it did constantly these days. She knew she had to make some drastic changes, and more than likely, a change in career was at the forefront. As much as she hated the thought of starting over and leaving behind her love for real estate, she couldn't think of an alternative.

Mentally exhausted, Sue let out a deep sigh as she turned out the lights and locked the office door. "Time to make some big changes, girl," she whispered to herself. "Like it or not, it may be time to move on."

Later that evening, when she couldn't seem to come up with a viable plan, Sue realized she was out of options. She had told herself she wouldn't involve Steve in her mess. After all, she had made her choices, and she shouldn't have to rely on her fiancé, or anyone else for that matter, to fix her life. Sue took great pride in her independence. She had always made her own way, even when that meant scraping by, working two jobs or doing whatever it took to pay her bills. Until now, she had always been successful. Joey's words kept ringing in her ears. She was going to have to admit it was time to talk to Steve, and see if he thought talking to Sean would help her the way it had helped him and Joey.

Stepping into the small area off the kitchen where Steve was working at the computer, Sue took a deep breath and pulled up a chair. "You have a minute?"

"Sure," Steve answered, as he continued typing. "What's up?"

"I've been thinking a lot about how well Joey is doing since he started at Sean's company."

"Yeah, I can't believe it. When you told me about that car, man.."

"Well," Sue gathered her thoughts. "Do you think it might be a good idea for me to talk to Sean? "

Steve finished his last sentence, saved his work, and turned to face Sue. "What do you mean?"

Sue turned her gaze toward the monitor. "Remember I told you it's been slow going working with Jenna?"

"Yeah?"

"Well," Sue looked down and nervously fingered the mouse pad. "It's been more than slow." Looking up at Steve, she admitted, "It's been miserable. I haven't sold a single property, and I don't even have any good leads. I feel like I'm a complete burden."

"Ah," Steve nodded. "You haven't been talking about work much, which is unusual, so I kind of wondered."

"Yeah. It's been tough. And the day I talked to Joey, right after I quit work, he suggested I talk to Sean. I didn't really think I needed to. I was sure I could do it on my own, but now.."

Steve leaned forward and grasped both of Sue's hands in his own. "Sue, I think it's a great idea. Working for an agency and working for yourself are two very different things that require different skills. Sean can definitely teach you the skills you need to succeed. He can teach me, while he's at it. He taught me all of the organizational skills I've used to get my work and home life under control. He taught Joey how to kill it in sales. I'd love to hear how he's so successful running his own business. Maybe he can teach you the secret to becoming a real estate tycoon!"

Sue laughed. "That would be great."

"He's going to be in town in a couple of weeks," Steve noted. "Coming out to check on the new company. I'm pretty sure Emily and the baby are coming with him. I'll give him a call and see if they'll have time to come over for dinner. I'll let him know you plan to pick his brain."

Leaning in to hug Steve, Sue smiled. For the first time in weeks she felt as if she had taken a step in the right direction.

Chapter 7

"Damn," Sue grumbled to herself. Staring at her online checking account, she couldn't believe the numbers staring back at her. After paying her half of the mortgage, bills, and the minimum payment on her credit card, there wasn't much left for anything else.

Her eyes wandered down to her savings account. The money she had been saving for the better part of five years. As soon as she had started working full-time, Sue had opened a savings account, expecting to use the money to buy a house. She had done exactly that when she and Steve had decided to move in together. Of course, without actually verbalizing it, she had also set aside what she thought of as a "wedding fund." Since she was a little girl, she had always dreamed of a big wedding, and she knew that if she wanted to carry out her dream, she'd better start putting away some money. Over time, the amount had grown, and Sue's dream had grown with it.

These past few months had taken more of a financial toll on Sue than she had realized. Paying for leads was easily responsible for 70% of her monthly spending. Leads that weren't getting her anywhere.

Now, all Sue could think about was having to liquidate her wedding fund just to make ends meet. The thought made her eyes fill with tears as she felt her dream slipping away.

"What's the matter?" Steve asked, entering the room and noticing the look on her face.

"Oh, nothing," Sue shook her head and logged out of her account. "Just the usual money issues. It's getting depressing."

"Well, I have some good news," Steve smiled. "I just got off the phone with Sean. They're going to be in town next week, so I invited them to dinner next Sunday. Actually, it'll be more of a late lunch since we all have early mornings, Monday." Laughing, he added, "Plus, Sean and I figured we can eat first, and then still catch part of the Superbowl."

"Great! Did you mention that I wanted to talk to Sean?"

"Yep. He's more than happy to talk to you about work and help you figure out how to drum up business. I explained to him a little bit of what's going on, but of course he'll want to hear it all from you. Get an idea of how you and Jenna are working together, how you find your leads, all of that."

"Thanks," Sue sighed. "I can't wait to hear what he has to say."

Chapter 8

"More wine?" Steve asked as he began to refill Emily's glass. "Thank you," she smiled. "And thank you both for having us over. This sure beats eating out every night."

"We're so glad you could make it," Sue said. "We've missed you guys since you left. And we finally got to meet Marty," she smiled as she grabbed the baby's hand, making him giggle.

Sean raised his glass in a toast and smiled. "To good friends, good fortune, and good times ahead!"

A resounding "Cheers!" filled the room as the four friends clinked glasses, laughing as Marty raised his hands and squealed in delight, including himself in the festivities.

"Well," Sean said, placing his glass on the table and turning toward Sue, "Let's get down to business. It's time to start 'Project Real Estate Mogul.'"

As everyone laughed, Steve stood up, wine glass in hand. "Come on, Emily. Why don't we introduce Marty to his first Superbowl. We haven't missed too much yet."

"Sounds good," she agreed, lifting the baby from his highchair.

Once the others had left the dining room, Sue grabbed a pen and notebook from the computer desk in the work area, returned to the table, and began to explain her situation to Sean.

"How's your relationship with Jenna surviving all this?" he asked.

"It's a little strained right now. She's been a great friend, and I can't blame her for being worried about the business. To be honest, I don't know what stresses me out more; being broke, or the thought of losing Jenna's friendship. I feel awful about everything."

"Well, let's see if we can change that," Sean offered.

"Please," Sue nodded. "You did such a great job with both Steve and Joey. They've both made such strides. I need to know what I'm doing wrong."

"I don't know that you're necessarily doing anything wrong," Sean reassured her. "I think you just need to focus on a few vital concepts. "

Sue nodded her agreement. "You don't seem to have had any trouble starting your business. It didn't even take you long to expand out here."

"No, this time around I knew how to do it right. One of the key differences between us is that before starting my business, I ensured I had enough savings to see it through. Of course, I had aspired to go into business for myself for several years, so I had planned accordingly. And it's a good thing I had, because the first time I tried, I ran into the same kind of trouble you're having."

"You did?" Sue asked, surprised.

"Absolutely. I had to shut down the first company I started, which was one of the most difficult decisions I've ever had to make."

"I can imagine," Sue said, shaking her head.

"I had to cut my losses and start the new business from the ground up. Of course, before doing that, I took a hard look at what I needed to do differently in order to succeed the next time around. One of my most important realizations was that in attempting to start a business, I had really just created another job for myself; not a business as I had intended."

Sue looked at Sean questioningly. "I don't think I understand the difference."

"Everything I teach you will be a factor in creating a business instead of another job. The way you look at your new situation will play a tremendous part in whether or not you succeed. In business, we look at what we call analogs and antilogs. Analogs are things that have worked in the past. Antilogs are the opposite; those are things that have failed. Are you with me?"

"I think so," Sue nodded, adding her first entry to the notebook.

"For instance, your former real estate agency surely had some good techniques that you would want to emulate. Those are your analogs. Practices that are tried and true, and would therefore be a good idea to bring with you to your new business."

"Makes sense," Sue agreed.

"On the other hand, I'm sure there are one or two things your old agency did that you probably found didn't work. Those are your antilogs. Analogs and antilogs are basically lessons; one is a lesson in how to succeed, while the other is a lesson in failure. Both are extremely useful when branching out on your own."

"Now, let me ask you a question," Sean continued. If you had the chance to do this over again, starting from scratch, what would you do differently?"

Sue stopped writing for a moment, and looked up. Sean could see the wheels turning in her mind, which was exactly what Sean was hoping. Getting Sue to sit down and start truly evaluating why her business wasn't succeeding was the first step in the right direction.

"You know," Sue responded, "I haven't really taken the time to think about that. I've been so focused on getting leads and trying to convert them to sales, I haven't stopped and thought about what changes I need to make to get myself off the ground." Sue shook her head and chuckled, "I know that sounds ridiculous, doesn't it?"

"Actually, no. It's very common for someone venturing out on their own to get so caught up in striving toward success, they forget to really create and follow a business plan. You'd be surprised at the high number of businesses that fail within the first year."

"Oh, I believe it," Sue said, eyebrows raised. "If nothing else, this experience has taught me how difficult it can be to branch out on your own. I mean, I figured with all of my experience in real estate, switching over from working for someone to working for myself would be a breeze."

"Yes, that's what most people think," Sean confirmed. "Unfortunately, being a subject matter expert makes you just that: an expert in your subject. And of course, while that's a huge plus, it doesn't have a whole lot to do with the success of running your business."

"I see that now," Sue agreed.

"What I recommend for anyone starting off on their own is what I call the 'Success Cloning Formula.' It's something I developed after my first business failed, and I realized I needed to take a different approach."

As Sue again began taking notes, Sean continued. "The formula is essentially a nine step guide to success. Much of it sounds like common sense, but surprisingly, many people, including myself, don't initially sit down and take the time to figure out what they need to do before jumping in feet first."

"Exactly what I did," Sue shook her head.

"It's natural. We want to get started right away, and common sense takes a back seat. In fact, surprisingly few people even follow step one, which is the most common sense step of all: setting a clear goal."

"Hmmm," Susan stopped writing and looked at Sean. "Isn't the goal to sell real estate a clear goal?"

"Well," Sean responded. "That's actually a very general goal. In the big picture, yes, that certainly is your overall goal. However, in order to determine whether or not you're meeting with the success you need to keep your business afloat, you need to be very clear about what you need to accomplish. For instance, maybe you want to start by setting a goal of getting 30 leads in the next 10 days. Once you're able to meet your initial goal, you aim a little higher. Eventually, when you find your rhythm, you may set a goal of selling one house a month."

"Got it," Sue nodded, as she turned to a fresh page in her notebook and continued writing. "Step 1: Setting a Clear Goal."

"Here," Sean stood up and walked to the desk where he had placed a folder he had brought with him. "I almost forgot I brought this."

Opening the folder, he removed a sheet of paper on which he had typed the formula. "I brought a copy for you. I keep one posted in my work area as a reminder; you know, in case I ever get off track."

"Thank you!" Sue eagerly took the paper and looked it over.

Success Cloning Formula

1) **Set a Clear Goal**
2) **Enumerate Reasons Behind this Goal**
3) **Find the Framework/Template**
4) **Create a Detailed Plan of Action**
5) **Implement a Mechanism to Deal with Setbacks**
6) **Self-Belief**
7) **Take Action**
8) **Review what Worked Well and what Did Not**
9) **Do More of what Works**

"I see what you mean," Sue said after a few minutes. "This is a good guide."

"Thank you," Sean smiled. "It's helped me quite a bit. Let's take a look at the second step. What are the reasons for your goal?"

"Well, working for myself is the main goal. Being able to be my own boss, set my own schedule, and be successful doing it, of course."

"Ok then, that's what you need to focus on," Sean said. "It

sounds as if autonomy is your main motivator. Freedom from working for anyone else."

"Exactly," Sue agreed.

"Then start with that. Whenever you feel overwhelmed or are tired of the struggle, remember the original reason you set out on your own. Remember how it felt working for someone who didn't appreciate you. How frustrating it was to not be able to spread your wings and do things your way. Imagine yourself running your own successful business, and the satisfaction of accomplishing more than you ever could, working for someone else. That's going to be your driving force. The framework, the plan of action.. all of it will come in time with a lot of thought, and a lot of trial and error. But never forget your reasons."

Sean words had brought Sue back in time. Particularly, back to her last, darkest day of work at her old firm. She remembered how Paul's words had stung. How shocked she had been at his accusations, and how empty she had felt walking out of the office for the last time. As if her past five years of hard work hadn't even happened. Just like that, it was all gone.

"I'm sure I'll never forget," Sue responded, sadly.

"Alright then," Sean nodded, seeing the look on Sue's face. "I definitely think it's the right time for you to be taking this step. You're ready. So let's start brainstorming the rest of this list."

With a renewed sense of purpose, Sue picked up her pen and started writing. She was ready, alright. She was motivated and ready to go. Then and there she decided the Success Cloning Formula was going to be the key to her new life.

Chapter 9

After meeting with Sean, Sue's hope was restored, and she was excited to get started with her new game plan. "Alright," she told herself. "Let's do this." She pulled out her notebook and began to review the goals she and Sean had come up with:

Step 1. 30 leads in 10 days.

Step 2. Start saving money.

Step 3. Ask friends and family for help with finding leads.

Step 4.

- List friends and family
- Make calls
- Ask each person for 5 contacts

Deciding step 4 was the best place to begin, Sue began making a list of who she thought would be the most willing and able to help her meet her goals. Starting with immediate and then extended family, she moved on to friends and former co-workers. With about 35 names on her list, Sue came to a standstill.

"Hmmm." Grabbing her phone, Sue did a quick scroll through her contact list, writing down names that hadn't immediately come to mind. Even though she hadn't spoken to these people in a while, she figured she'd give them a call and see if they might be willing to help.

Putting down her phone, Sue reached for her computer and pulled up her email account. There were another fifty or so contacts she could try to reach through email. Again, she hadn't been in contact with many of them lately, but what the heck; she figured it was worth a shot.

Finally, Sue pulled up her Facebook page. "Ok," she thought to herself. "I have a zillion Facebook friends, but very few phone numbers or email addresses for them."

"Well," she sighed, "let me get started with these phone calls."

One by one, Sue placed calls to everyone on her contact list, only to be met with disappointment. Her most promising contacts turned out to be her immediate family members and closest friends. These were the people who were excited to learn about her new endeavors and cheer her on. Even though it didn't sound as if many of them currently had friends in the market, they asked about Sue's new business and promised to pass her information on to their own friends and families.

Unfortunately, the majority of the calls Sue made didn't pan out at all. A large number of them went to voicemail, while an equally significant number of them went nowhere at all. "Figures," she thought as she got yet another automated message telling her the number she had dialed was out of service. "That's what I get for losing touch with people."

Sue left messages for those with voice mail, and followed up each message with a text. While it was a time consuming task, she hoped it would be worth the effort.

Once she had finished attempting to contact people via telephone, Sue moved on to her email connections, hoping for better luck than she'd had with the phone.

Sue had just started sending emails when Steve arrived home from work.

"Hey," he said, coming through the door. "How'd it go today?"

"Not so great," Sue shook her head as he crossed the room and gave her a kiss on the cheek. "I didn't have as much luck making phone calls as I'd hoped. I'm starting on emails, but it's taking forever. And I don't even know if most of these addresses are even valid. It's been so long since I've communicated with these people."

Pulling up a chair next to her, Steve looked at her screen. "Oh, you can't possibly send an individual email to every contact you have!"

"Well, I created a standard message and am copying and pasting it to everyone, so it isn't as time consuming."

"No, no, no," Steve shook his head. "There's a great program called 'Mail Chimp.' If you go to mailchimp.com, you can personalize an email template. It's personal, so it makes your email look as if it were sent specifically to each person. You can send it to like 2000 people at a time, and it's free!"

"Are you serious?" Sue looked at Steve with wide eyes. "That's amazing!"

"Yeah. And the best part is you can see exactly who received and opened your email. That way, when you notice someone has opened it, you can follow up right away."

"Ok, I'm going to do that right now. Thanks!"

"No problem." Steve stood up and started to loosen his tie. "I'm going to go change and flop on the sofa for a while. Let me know how it goes."

"Will do," Sue answered as she got started with her new email project.

Chapter 10

"What's wrong?" Steve asked Sue over dinner a few weeks later, noticing she didn't seem to be her usual, talkative self.

"I'm just frustrated," Sue said, picking at her food. "I made a zillion phone calls, sent text messages, and sent another zillion emails, and I still feel like I'm not getting anywhere. Oh, I even sent a bunch of messages on Facebook to people whose contact information I don't have."

"What kind of a response did you get?"

"Not much of anything. Some polite replies, but no real leads. Most people didn't respond at all."

"It's only been a couple of weeks," Steve reminded her.

"It's been more than three. I checked, and a lot of people opened the emails. They just didn't bother to respond. I spent some time sending follow up emails to the ones who opened them, and that didn't work so well either."

"That is frustrating," Steve agreed.

"And I'm mad at myself. I had a few leads that Jenna had given me. Between trying to follow up with all of this, and spending a lot of time with one client in particular that seemed real serious about buying a house I had shown him, it took me a little over a week to make contact with the others."

"What happened?"

"Once I called them back, one of them had changed her mind and decided not to buy right now, and the other two had already moved on to different agents."

"Ah, that sucks. I'm sorry." Steve reached across the table and took Sue's hand in his.

"It's my fault. I need to figure out how to get organized and use my time more wisely."

Steve squeezed Sue's hand reassuringly. "The good news is Sean is coming back to town in a little over a week. He's already told me he wants to see you and hear how you're doing."

Sue smiled. "That's great news. I just wish I had better things to report."

"Don't worry," Steve laughed. "After dealing with me, he's seen it all. If he could get me on track, you won't be any trouble."

Sue nodded and laughed. "That's true. I guess there's hope after all."

Chapter 11

"Thank you so much for making time to meet with me," Sue smiled over her cup of coffee.

"Not at all," Sean returned. "I've been anxious to hear how the formula has been working for you. I was sorry to hear it hasn't been going all that well. Remember though, it's only been two months."

"True," Sue nodded.

"So tell me. What are some of the changes you've made since we last spoke? What I'm really looking for are things you've done that you feel have worked well for you, or that have earned you praise from others."

Sue opened her notebook and turned to her list of achievements. "One thing I did, which Jenna really liked, was create a Facebook page for the business."

"That's great! What sort of information do you have on there, aside from the basics?"

"Well, I have a question and answer section that has gotten a lot of 'likes.' I reached out to friends and family, and asked what types of questions they'd had when they were in the process of buying or selling a home. Jenna also supplied me with a number of questions her clients have asked her throughout the years, so I posted the most commonly asked questions, along with their answers."

"Have you noticed a marked improvement in business since posting that?" Sean asked, sipping his coffee.

"No," Sue admitted. "I get a lot of positive feedback on the site, and I've gotten a few new leads because of it, but none of them have converted to a sale."

"Regardless, you're on the right track," Sean assured her. "Facebook is a fantastic tool to promote a business. Your idea to post questions and answers is also an excellent one. Have you marketed yourself on other social media sites, such as Linkedin and Twitter?"

"No," Sue shook her head. "But I probably should."

"Absolutely. The idea is to get your business out there any way you can. All of these sites are free, so you aren't spending a dime on marketing. And the following they have is incredible."

"Now," Sean continued, "I want to talk to you about two important tactics you need to consider. The first one is positioning your service."

"I know what you mean by that," Sue commented as she began taking notes. "I remember when Jenna was in the process of opening her business, she made a point of positioning herself in an upscale area. It has made a difference in the clientele. We definitely attract wealthier clients in that area than we did at my previous agency."

"Exactly. It sounds as if Jenna decided she wanted to target a specific clientele, and opening the business where she did made that possible. Have you ever heard of Joshua Bell?"

"No," Sue stopped writing and tilted her head in interest.

"He's one of the most renowned classical violinists in the world. He plays a Stradivarius violin which was built in 1713, is known to be the most beautiful sounding violin ever created, and is currently valued at $3.5 million. Bell played in a Boston concert hall one evening, and earned over $60,000 per hour."

"Wow!" Sue exhaled.

"Yeah, pretty impressive. Now, at the height of his career, only a few days after his performance in the Boston concert hall, Mr.

Bell was asked by the Washington Post to participate in an experiment. He was asked to play the violin at a local subway station for one hour, where thousands of people would pass through and hear his music. So, on January 12, 2007, Bell arrived at the subway station, set up shop, and opened his violin case as an invitation to anyone who cared to make a donation. After an hour of playing a list of classical masterpieces for an hour on this beautiful violin worth millions of dollars, can you guess how much the finest violinist in the world had made?"

"No idea," Sue shook her head.

"Thirty two dollars."

"What?" Sue gasped, mouth open.

"That's right. This world famous musician, playing the same music on the same violin, earned $32 an hour in one instance, and $60,000 per hour in another. What was the key factor?"

"Positioning," Sue answered. "That's amazing."

"It sure is," Sean agreed. "But it goes to show, how you position yourself, and in turn, the type of clientele you attract, makes all the difference. Of course, it goes without saying that if you're going to position yourself in a concert hall, you'd better be able to deliver. The same goes with your business. Positioning yourself in an upscale area is a good move. But, the types of clients you're going to attract in that location are going to have higher expectations. You follow me?"

"I think so."

"So what are some of the things you can do to meet the expectations of your clients?"

Sue put down her pen and took a moment to consider Sean's question. "Well, I know they value their time greatly."

"Good answer. Time is money."

"So," Sue went on, "I need to make sure they don't feel as if I'm wasting their time."

"Bingo," Sean raised a finger in the air, making a point. "That's a primary concern for anyone. These folks are obviously success-ful, and didn't meet with success by wasting anyone's time, or their own. And you won't either."

"I probably need to be more flexible with my office hours. I've been trying to work mostly between nine and five, but of course I take appointments for later in the evening."

"Would you consider instead of appointments, being readily available when your phone rings? I know it's inconvenient, but what if a client calls you at eight in the evening, maybe even on a Saturday evening, and wants to run over and see a property then and there? Would you be able to oblige?"

"I suppose I could," Sue replied, a bit reluctantly. "But it might be sort of hard to have a life of my own if I get in the habit of doing that."

"That's true," Sean agreed. "But, it isn't something you'll have to do forever. It's a way to build up a customer base, by showing clients you're serious about selling, and are willing to put their needs first. Once you have some loyal customers who are referring you to their family and friends, your immediate availability won't be the primary focus for them. You'll have established yourself as a trustworthy, dedicated agent, and that reputation will surpass the need to be available at the drop of a hat."

"I get it. I just need a way to get people's attention so I can prove myself to them."

"Exactly. I'm willing to bet most of the established realtors in that area aren't available at all hours. You'll be meeting a need that likely isn't being met, which is another criterion in positioning yourself. Once you have a solid clientele, you can continue to ful-fill this need by offering a flexible schedule. You don't have to be available every Saturday night or Sunday morning, but maybe you can make yourself available two nights a week until 8 pm, and one Saturday a month from, say, 6 am until 9 pm. Just an example, but by offering something other agents typically don't, you'll set yourself apart from the rest."

"That wouldn't be so bad," Sue agreed as she wrote down Sean's suggestion.

"Ok, so we have making the most of the client's time while you have them, which is a given, as well as offering flexible hours that other realtors may not offer. What else do you think would appeal to the client that they may not be getting from other agents?"

Once again taking a moment to gather her thoughts, Sue finished off her coffee. "You know, at my last agency, I was always surprised we never had an online portal for clients. I've seen some of the more sophisticated companies' portals, and they're fantastic. They allow the potential buyer to log on anytime they want and see exactly what's on the market in their price range, in any of the locations they're considering. These portals offer detailed information about each property, including extensive photographs. They set the parameters themselves, can create multiple searches, and can even sign up to have the system send them daily or weekly emails based on the searches they've created. The portals feed directly from the MLS, so new properties appear immediately without the agent having to do a single thing. It's a great tool for the agent, because the client can essentially find his or her own home without any help. It saves time for the realtor, and at the same time gives the client a great sense of freedom; they don't have to wait for the realtor to show them something."

"That sounds great," Sean replied. "But what's the difference between a portal like that and the client just using a site like Trulia or Redfin?"

"Those sites are helpful," Sue responded, "but often, the homes listed on those sites are already pending. Many of them aren't actually available, but the site doesn't always offer that information. Usually, the home will appear as available until it's actually sold and the deal has been closed."

"I see. So the realtor's portal specifies which homes are truly available and which are contingent?"

"Yes. I've had clients become very frustrated when they get excited over a home they've found online, only to call me and discover it already has multiple offers."

"Well, then," Sean smiled. "I think you've just come up with a tremendous way to set yourself head and shoulders above the average realtor. Just recently, Emily and I bought our home back east. We went through exactly what you described. We would find something online that seemed to fit our needs perfectly. Unfortunately, by the time we got in touch with our realtor, the house already had at least one offer. We would sometimes put in a backup offer, and that is eventually how we got our house, but it was incredibly frustrating. We would have killed to have a portal we could search on our own, and know that what we saw actually was still up for grabs. I hated waiting for our agent to email or call us about homes she had found that she thought we might like. Obviously, she had a lot of clients, and could only get to us when she had time. I remember getting very annoyed with her at one point, asking how other people were able to find and buy these homes so quickly, when by the time we saw them, they were already sold. It makes sense. If we'd had access to a realtor's portal, we could have been actively searching on our own, and beating others to the punch."

"You're right," Sue said. "I can't believe I didn't think of that immediately. And the portal is really cool in that the realtor sees everything the client is doing. So, it allows the realtor to see if the client has become interested in a new area, or if they've started taking a peek at properties they previously insisted were out of their price range. And of course, if a client hasn't been active lately, it's a good sign they may need a push. Or, if a previous client who dropped out the search is suddenly back and looking, it's time to make a phone call and follow up with them to see if they're back in the game."

"That truly is awesome," Sean nodded. "Do you guys have a website?"

"No. That's the first thing we need to get done. The website will direct the client to the portal."

"My suggestion would be to have it done professionally. It isn't cheap, but it's money well spent. Make sure the professional setting it up makes it extremely user friendly. That's another factor of positioning. If it takes too long for clients to figure it out, they're going to move on. Remember, time is valuable. Nobody wants to spend their time fighting with a website, trying to figure out how to get into your portal. It should be a quick point and click, and that's it."

"Got it," Sue noted, writing furiously. "These are a lot of really good ideas. I'm starting to get excited!"

"You should be excited," Sean smiled. "You're on fire!"

"I sure hope so," Sue laughed. "Ok, so those are great ideas for positioning the business. You said you had two important tactics."

"Yes. The other is pretty simple. I just want you to start thinking outside the box."

"Makes sense," Sue nodded. "But help me think of how."

"I know you told me you've been getting leads from Jenna, purchasing them from agencies, and also from friends and family."

"Well, I've been trying to get them from friends and family, but I haven't had much luck there. My friends and family don't seem to know a lot of people in the market right now."

"Understandable," Sean said. "The market isn't terrific right now. But what I would suggest is looking in other directions. For instance, is Jenna a broker?"

"Yes," Sue affirmed. "I'm working under her until I get my broker's license. Then I'll be able to work completely independently, like she does."

"Ok, so as a broker, chances are she has a close relationship with other brokers in the field. She probably turned to them for help when she was starting out."

"That's right. She's mentioned a few of them who really helped her get her feet off the ground."

"See, people like that, who are our mentors, are often willing to continue helping us for the long haul. I bet if she placed some calls, they'd be happy to refer some clients to you guys, knowing Jenna has a new person on board."

"I didn't even think of that," Sue said. "I don't think Jenna did, either. It sure would beat paying for all our leads."

"Sure. Also, you must have worked with photographers and professional stagers who stage houses."

"Yes, I have a few friends who do that. I used to refer my clients to them to dress up their homes after they had moved out. Homes professionally staged with furniture and some art work always sell more quickly than homes without."

"Well there you have it," Sean opened his hands in an expression of success. "You got business for them; I bet they'd be willing to return the favor. Why not contact some of your friends in the staging business and see if they know of any good prospects?"

"That's a thought," Sue agreed.

"You know, not to be morbid, but you could even check the obituaries now and then. County records might show if the deceased owned a home. Obviously you'd have to use discretion, but sometimes the relatives who inherited the property are eager to sell rather than deal with it."

Sue chuckled at the thought. "That really is thinking outside the box."

"It is," Sean smiled. "But when it comes to business, you really do have to explore every avenue. Also, what percentage do you charge the seller?"

"Six percent is pretty standard. If I work with another realtor, we split it."

"Just a thought. Many years ago, when I was getting ready to move from San Diego to L.A., I needed to sell my condo to buy a house. I had a certain amount of money I knew I needed to walk away with in order to be able to make a down payment. The market had gone up a bit, but it was still fairly hard to sell at the time. I knew I would make some money, but I wasn't sure how much. My realtor and I had decided on a listing price. After a month or so, I lowered the price a bit. Another month went by, and I'd had a few offers, but all of them had fallen through. I lowered it again, and again had a few offers that didn't pan out. Finally, my agent came up with a buyer who was very serious. He loved my condo, but couldn't quite get approved for the asking price. He was approved for just about $2000 below. I was extremely hesitant to lower the price again because I knew what I had to make to buy the house I wanted. My realtor told me if I lowered the price, she would lower her fees by .5%. This allowed me to lower the price so the buyer could make an offer, and I still walked away with exactly what I needed. To this day, when anyone I know needs a realtor in San Diego, I give them her name. What she did showed me that she put her clients first. It showed her motivation to make a sale, and to keep the client, me, happy."

"That is an amazing story," Sue shook her head. "And not something you hear of often. I can tell she left a lasting impression on you."

"I'm not saying it's something you want to do all the time, but when the market is tough, it might not be a bad way to go. Talk about building customer loyalty."

"I can imagine," Sue nodded, still in awe. "I certainly wouldn't be against doing something like that. Obviously it pays off in the long run."

"Sure does," Sean agreed.

Smiling, Sue closed her notebook. "Well, I don't want to take up any more of your time. You've given me a lot to think about. I have to say, I have an entirely new outlook right now. I can't wait to talk to Jenna and share some of these ideas."

"I'm really excited for you, Sue. I see great things in your future."

As Sean stood up, Sue grabbed her things, walked around the table and gave him a quick hug. "I can't wait until the next time you're in town. I have a feeling this time the story is going to have a happy ending."

Chapter 12

Since her second meeting with Sean, Sue's ambition and outlook had been restored. Realizing she needed to follow the formula much more closely, Sue was determined to carefully consider each step before setting her plans into motion. She told herself she needed to patiently await the results and make sure she was making progress before advancing to the next step.

The first thing Sue did was start with another mass email. The lack of response to her last email was an eye-opener. She realized that even though most of the people on her contact list were friends and acquaintances, they were busy like everyone else. Taking the time to find leads for Sue probably wasn't at the top of their "to-do" lists.

This time, instead of simply informing her contacts of her new business and asking for leads, she decided to try a new tactic. Rather than asking for help, Sue decided to give her contacts the opportunity to ask questions about the real estate process. Because the question and answer section of her Facebook page had been such a success, it was evident people were interested in learning about real estate practices.

"What is the number one question you have about buying or selling real estate in this economy?" Sue wrote. As she had hoped, this simple strategy resulted in almost three times as many responses as her previous email. Although many of the responses made it clear they were not currently in the market, they still had questions, "just in case" their situation changed in the future. In other words, Sue's email had started a conversation, and had gotten people with no intention of selling or buying property to begin seeing it as a possibility.

Sue responded to every question within a 24 hour period so as to not waste anyone's time, and to demonstrate her dedication. She used a combination of her own expertise, as well as research conducted online, to offer the most thorough responses possible. Evidently her contacts were more interested in the prospect of getting into the market than they thought they were, because Sue noticed once she had answered a question, her contacts would respond with several more.

After a few weeks had passed and Sue had gotten a strong response to her email, she decided it was time to move forward. Realizing that if a simple email could draw so much interest, a video might be even more provocative. Using her cell phone, Sue recorded a simple promotional video:

> *Hey everyone! Your real estate agent, Sue here! A lot of you have been asking questions about buying and selling real estate in today's market. Hopefully I've been able to address most of your concerns. Even in this challenging economy, there are ways to get the most for your home. People are still buying, and some simple, fairly inexpensive upgrades can raise your home's value and make it very competitive. And of course, those of you in the market to buy can rest assured I will help you find exactly what you're looking for, and get you the most bang for your buck. With my years of real estate experience and my numerous contacts in the field, I guarantee there is no roadblock we can't overcome together. I look forward to answering all of your questions, and serving you with the trustworthy, loyal service that is my trademark. Please feel free to use the information at the bottom of the screen to contact me via telephone, email, or Facebook. I will always respond within 24 hours. I look forward to hearing from you, and beginning this exciting journey together.*

Sue felt the video was a success in that it was only slightly over 2 minutes long, yet presented a gentle, but firm call to action. Because she had proven to herself she could respond to everyone's emails within 24 hours and that seemed to impress her contacts, she decided that would be her rule of thumb, and hopefully something that would set her apart from other realtors. By taking just a few minutes every so often throughout the day to check her email, phone, and Facebook messages, Sue would be able to get an idea of how much time she would need to set aside for responses, and thereby plan her day and evening accordingly.

Once the video was completed to her satisfaction, Sue used every free resource she could think of to promote it; resources which also happened to draw a massive audience. She posted the video on her personal Facebook page, the Facebook page she had created for the business, and YouTube. Finally, she sent one more mass email to her contact list, and attached the video. Now that she felt she had gotten the attention of her contacts through her question and answer emails, she suspected they would take the time to watch her video.

Sure enough, by the following day, Sue had received an overwhelmingly positive response to her video. Potential clients had sent her messages on Facebook. Others had responded to her emails asking questions, and telling her they had forwarded her video to friends, family members, or colleagues who were looking for a realtor. She even received messages from folks who had seen her video on YouTube, and wanted to schedule a meeting with her for more information.

Sue had to pinch herself to make sure she wasn't dreaming. With just a few simple steps and attention to detail, she had accomplished her goal. In a few short weeks, Sue had effectively established herself as a leading real estate expert in her area.

Chapter 13

"It's great to see you," Sean said as he hugged Sue, and then sat down with his coffee at their favorite table.

"You too," Sue smiled.

"I have to say, you look much happier than the last time I saw you."

"I am," Sue grinned. "I followed your plan to a 'T' this time, and wow."

"Success?"

"More than I had ever anticipated. I have so many clients, I can barely keep up. I've of course given a number of them to Jenna as a thank you for everything she's done for me, and she's thrilled. We've both been closing on homes at a fantastic rate. And in this market!"

"You go girl!" Sean exclaimed, raising his hand for a fist bump. "Absolutely tremendous. So tell me.. what is it you did differently this time around?"

"You know," Sue began. "That's the thing that kills me. You were right when you said I wasn't actually doing anything wrong. It was all about fine tuning what I was already doing."

Sean sipped his coffee and nodded, clearly intrigued.

"For instance, the mass emails I sent out turned out to be extremely effective; but only after I started offering the clientele an opportunity to take the lead. I asked them what *they* wanted to know about real estate and placed the ball in their court. I had to force myself to lay off selling myself for a while. I know there's a time and a place for that, but not until you've established yourself in their eyes as someone who is worthy of doing business with them."

"Very true," Sean nodded. "Until you establish yourself as a knowledgeable source and someone in whom they can place their trust, trying to sell yourself is like running into a brick wall over and over. It offers nothing in return except a headache."

"I learned that pretty quickly," Sue agreed. "While I was doing research, I stumbled across an article about farming vs. hunting. The author discussed running a business where he had to catch butterflies for a living. Initially, he was running around with butterfly nets, trying to catch them with little success. Eventually he realized if he built a beautiful garden filled with plants and flowers, the butterflies would be drawn to it on their own. It finally clicked with me that I was doing the same thing; I was chasing down clients as if they were prey. In reading this guy's story, I flashed back to what you said about positioning yourself. In the author's case, that meant creating a sanctuary for butterflies. In my case, it translated into turning myself into the local expert in my field. Once I was able to do that, clients started knocking down my door as opposed to the other way around."

"That's a fantastic analogy," Sean said, eyebrows raised. "I'm impressed."

"Thank you," Sue smiled. "Reading that story actually made me feel better knowing I wasn't the only one who started off with the wrong mindset. One of the most important things I did was take the time to conduct my weekly reviews. I was able to take a hard look at what was and wasn't working, and change things accordingly. When I realized there were certain questions I couldn't answer, I spent my free time, back when I still had some, researching and learning everything I could about California real estate laws. I created my own question and answer database for personal reference, making it easier and much quicker to respond to clients."

"Good thinking. Every state has different laws, and they can be confusing. California, being one of the most transient states, will always have people new to the area that are going to rely on you to answer their questions."

"Very true," Sue nodded. "So once I finally understood the concept of drawing people to me through my expertise, I decided I needed to learn to promote myself in a professional forum. I knew I had a lot to offer, and didn't want to lessen my value through poor marketing."

"Very good," Sean confirmed. "Knowing your stuff is critical, but without good marketing, it does you no good."

"Right. So I did more research, this time exploring people who were experts in the field of online marketing. Even though they weren't necessarily in the field of real estate, I knew they would have a lot of tools I could use, and they did. For instance, LinkedIn was a site that kept popping up. I'd always heard it could be a useful means to form business connections, so I spent some time learning to navigate it. I signed up for a premium account with them which allows me to use the InMail feature. It's a great way to contact prospects in my area."

"Yes," Sean nodded. "I love LinkedIn. It's a great tool."

"Me too. I created a standard message template to use when someone adds me as a contact on LinkedIn. Take a look:"

Dear <prospectname>,

Thank you for connecting with me! I am writing to ask if you would be interested in meeting with me to discuss mutual business interests.

I understand you might need help with property investments.

I help investors find the right property to invest in for the long term and I also give them exit recommendations based on their goals.

<prospectname>, I would also be happy to connect you with any of my contacts in my network if you think they would be able to help you with your business.

Thank you again for connecting with me. I look forward to hearing from you.

Sincerely,

Sue Amadori

Email

Website

Phone

"I like that!" Sean smiled. "Very professional."

"I figure I can use that template to secure buyers since I'm focusing on sellers in some other ways."

"Like what?"

"I crafted an offer to give potential sellers an attractive, low-risk way of doing business with me. Since I'm not paying for leads anymore, I decided to re-direct that money toward offering sellers a free valuation of their property. That way, even if the seller is indecisive and not in a hurry to take action, the offer of a free valuation seems to get them moving. If the valuation turns out to be higher than they had anticipated, they tend to want to move forward before the market starts to slip. Basically, I've positioned myself as the resident expert, and created a sense of urgency by advertising only 10 free valuations available per month. I could go over that number if I needed to, but I've noticed that setting a limit makes my phone ring off the hook."

"Brilliant!" Sean exclaimed. "I love it!"

"Thanks! Here, take a look at the email I created for sellers:"

Why do I need a market valuation for my property?

As real estate experts will tell you, the key to selling or renting property at its highest value in the shortest amount of time is to get an accurate valuation so you know exactly how much it's worth.

We will not only valuate your property, but will also advise you on factors that may work for or against you when you decide to sell or rent your property.

Is there a catch to this FREE valuation? Absolutely not. This is a non-obligatory service, and you owe us nothing in return.

What's in it for me, you ask?

Our core staff has over twenty years of experience. Our knowledge and expertise is an invaluable asset geared toward understanding your needs and devising the best marketing and negotiation strategies for you, if you do decide to sell. By choosing us, you can rest assured you have made the best decision for you and your property.

How do I get this FREE, NO-OBLIGATION service?
Simply follow the steps below:

1) Click on the link in this email.
2) Enter your name, phone number, preferred time slot, and email in the form provided.

That's it!

We will call you at your preferred time and set up an appointment for your free property valuation.

"Sue, this is absolutely fantastic," Sean marveled.

"Thank you! When they click on the link in the email, they end up at a very simple, professionally developed website, as you suggested. The website has an 'opt in' box, or a 'lead capture' box. If the client chooses to enter their information, they'll receive a PDF download detailing our services, some basic questions and answers, that sort of thing. Hopefully being sent to the site also encourages them to snoop around a little and read more about us, see our success stories, and all the other good stuff we have going on."

Sue laughed at herself. "I think I'm talking your ear off. I could go on and on about long-tailed keywords, squeeze pages, pay per click ads, auto-responders.. all the things I've learned to do since I started following the Success Cloning Formula. I can't thank you enough for all you've done."

"No, you did this yourself, Sue. I'm so proud of you."

Raising her coffee cup in a toast, Sue smiled. "Here's to you, my friend."

Sean returned Sue's toast, shaking his head and laughing. "No, this toast is to *you*, Sue. From now on, I'll be coming to you for advice. I do believe the student has become the master."

Chapter 14

We have all heard the clichés about Success. One that keeps coming up every now and then is, "Success is a journey, not a destination."

When you are working hard in life, success seems like the ultimate destination. It may be your goal to live in a breathtaking mansion, spend holidays traveling to exotic lands, or simply have the corner office. But, when you finally fulfill your dream, does it actually give you the satisfaction you once thought it would? People who are perceived as successful by others actually feel that success is more of a phase: short-lived and subject to change.

This change can be for the better or worse. The feeling of greatness after having achieved what you always hoped for does not quite live up to your expectations. Sometimes, you feel like you have achieved something huge, and then that feeling vanishes. One thing we have learned about success is that it is not a destination, but a continual process. If you truly want to be happy and successful, you must appreciate all the twisting paths, hills, and valleys on the route to success – because success is the route itself!

On the other hand, there are people like Sue who set out on a certain path, but find that the path is not what they thought it would be!

This book has been written to cater to both of these audiences. This book is not about how to start a business; there are plenty of books that teach you how to do that. This book is about the Success Cloning Formula, at which we have arrived by studying the lives and biographies of successful people. We have distilled all of this information into a simple framework.

A framework is simply a basic structure or system for accomplishing something. Think about it. If we drop you off at a junkyard and say, "Hey, do us a favor. Go pick up all the pieces required to make a running car, put them together, and drive that vehicle out of there."

Would you be able to do that? Without a framework, probably not.

"To live through an impossible situation, you don't need to have the reflexes of a Grand Prix driver, the muscles of a Hercules, the mind of an Einstein. You simply need to know what to do."

– Anthony Greenback

We like this quote by Anthony Greenback. If only we knew what to do!

Step 3 of the formula refers to finding the framework/template. So where does one go to find the relevant framework/ template? There are several options.

1) **Find a mentor who has already done what you want to do, and ask them what their framework was.**

   Mentors play a critical role in our daily lives. A mentor can us help make important decisions such as choosing the best career path to complement our skills and personality, decide whether relocating might be of benefit, and even consider which job offers to entertain.

2) **Research your topic.**

   When you decide to forge your path, form a habit of reading, because that's the way to get smarter. Reading books written by others who have accomplished what you hope to achieve not only provides guidance, but is an excellent way to maintain your enthusiasm toward your goal. If someone else has reached their dream, you can do it to! Read the excerpts on Amazon before you make a decision on which book best fits your needs.

3) Google it!

There is a treasure trove of lectures and Q&A's on the internet. Just search for known industry leaders and scholars, and find out what they have to say about your situation.

4) Find mentors in different industries from your own, and see if you can apply what they teach to your own industry.

5) Find Analogs and figure out how they did things differently.

6) Find Antilogs and figure out what you should not do.

7) Start associating with people who share your interests.

You can get a clear picture of what a particular career entails, as well as the demands of the job, by observing people already working in that field. Combine that with the information you have, your doubts and reservations, and allow people to advise you. This way, you can avoid common mistakes others have already made.

8) Find friends who are searching too.

A friend can inspire enthusiasm as well as accountability, and that serves to challenge you. Spend time with people who are also in transition, and compare notes. The more interested you are in other people, the more they'll reveal to you.

Step 4 of the formula refers to creating a Detailed Plan of Action

Oftentimes, we get bogged down when we are faced with the prospect of writing down an action plan. An action plan is simply a sequence of steps that must be taken, or activities that must be performed well, for a strategy to succeed.

An action plan has three major elements:

1) Specific tasks: what will be done and by whom.
2) Time horizon: when will it be done.
3) Resource allocation: what specific funds are available for specific activities.

If you still feel stuck, simply look at the framework/template you have created and expand on it.

Step 5 of the formula is Implementing a Mechanism to Deal with Setbacks

Setbacks are to be expected on the road to success. They are usually considerations, fears or roadblocks.

Considerations and fears are mainly internal, and are caused by our emotions. Emotions play an immense role in decision-making; hence they should not be ignored. However, making emotional decisions can lead to negative outcomes, something that most of us do not anticipate.

On the other hand, there are roadblocks which sometimes block our way. Roadblocks are external circumstances that get in the way of what we want. Never forget that there is always more than one way to do something. You can go over the roadblock, around the roadblock, or you can tunnel through the block. Most people simply give up when they face a roadblock and return right to the road from which they came. Even when you can't go straight, remember you can turn left or turn right, and find an alternate route to your destination.

It is important to think ahead and plan for these setbacks. Don't just hope for the best. Have a plan ready for things that you could reasonably expect to go wrong, and if they do, simply execute that plan!

Here is a simple plan to deal with setbacks:

1st Step: Awareness

Concentrate fully on whatever it is you are trying to do. Bad decisions are made when you allow yourself to lose focus. This can be difficult when life insists on getting in the way. Work and home life take up most of our thoughts and energy. Keep in mind, your very reason for following your dream is to improve upon both of those. It's imperative to make time to work toward your goal, and keep your eye on the prize.

2nd Step: Always think of an option, a Plan B

When you are aware and focused, you will not forget that you have the option to make different choices. How you behave is your choice.

3rd Step: Trust the option you go with

The knowledge that you have the power to choose should help you to trust yourself to opt for the right decision.

4th Step: Whatever decision you make, own it!

Accepting your decision to behave in a certain manner, whether good or bad, is a big step in admitting you are human. If there is something you can do about a setback, do it; but if you can't, learn your lesson and focus on what you can do to change things.

5th Step: Focus on the future

When one moment passes, another begins. Such is life. You should therefore make a constant decision to move forward. Live the present moment, and continue focusing on your success framework.

6th Step: Self Belief

The pressure of wandering off the beaten path and going against the tide can take its toll. The pressure to choose and stick to an unknown path can often have you feeling cornered and frustrated. Most people give up when the going gets tough. Self-belief can be the difference between a successful person and an unsuccessful one.

Developing Self-Belief

There are three ways to develop self-belief that work especially well:

1) Remember your past accomplishments.
2) Avoid comparing yourself to others.
3) Develop yourself.

It is this combination of developing yourself, challenging yourself, and deliberately thinking about yourself in more constructive ways, that represents the ideal recipe for building self-belief.

7th Step: Taking Action.

Here are some ways you can grow the action habit:

1) Don't wait until conditions are perfect.
2) Start small.
3) Use action to cure fear.
4) Set a schedule for your actions.

8th Step: The Review

Question 1: What Went Well?

In the quest to make improvements, it's natural to focus on pain points: things that didn't go well. But asking ourselves what went well, allows us to acknowledge all the good things that have happened, too.

Question 2: What Didn't Go So Well?

The intention of this question is to identify and unearth difficulties, issues and dissatisfactions with the process. Where better to look to make improvements than where things are not going well?

Question 3: What Have I Learned?

This is a powerful question, and reflecting on it tends to open our minds to things of which we might not otherwise take notice. It encourages us to look at what we've learned about the way we're working.

Question 4: What Still Puzzles Me?

Puzzles and open questions express a question we have – a gap in our knowledge. This question liberates us to express things we wish we had the answers for, but don't. A question is more likely than a statement to foster thoughts, insights, and a positive outcome from everyone involved.

9th Step: Do more of what works

Life is pretty simple: You do some stuff. Most fails. Some works. You do more of what works. If it works big, others quickly copy it. Then you do something else. The trick is the doing something else.

– Tom Peters

Conclusion

There's so much success advice out there, and some of it seems to be contradictory. With this book, we have stripped away the non-essentials and tried to give you a framework that you can apply to any situation. We'll leave the deciding up to you.

You've now learned the entire system — what it is, why it works, and how it works. Now it's time to put it to use in your own life and business.

To help get you up and running quickly, here's a simple three-step action plan:

Step 1: Figure out what you want to do.

Step 2: Follow the Success Cloning Formula, even if you are unsure about the framework/template

Step 3: Review what worked and revise the framework/template every week.

There may be setbacks, but there are also solutions to the problems that arise. With some dedication, motivation and a disciplined approach, you will be able to bounce back from any setback.

We wish you all the best in your life journey!